*Let your crystal journey begin...*

Copyright © 2020 Purple Parrot Publishing

The right of Purple Parot Publishing to be identified as the author and designer has been asserted in accordance with the Copyright, Designs and Patents Act 1988.

All rights reserved. No part of this publication may be reproduced, stored in a retrieval system, or transmitted, in any form or by any means (electronic, mechanical, photocopying, recording or otherwise), without the prior written permission of the publisher.

Published by Purple Parrot Publishing

Printed in the United Kingdom

First Printing, 2020

ISBN:   Print:   978-1-912677-63-4

Purple Parrot Publishing

www.purpleparrotpublishing.co.uk

Purple Parrot
Publishing

*This Notebook belongs to*

..................................

# Colour me...

www.ingramcontent.com/pod-product-compliance
Lightning Source LLC
Chambersburg PA
CBHW071348080526
44587CB00017B/3022